CHARLIE BROWN FAVORITES

15 SELECTIONS ARRANGED BY PHILLIP KEVEREN

— PIANO LEVEL —
LATE INTERMEDIATE/EARLY ADVANCED

© 2018 PEANUTS Worldwide LLC
www.snoopy.com

ISBN 978-1-5400-2106-9

7777 W. BLUEMOUND RD. P.O. BOX 13819 MILWAUKEE, WI 53213

In Australia Contact:
Hal Leonard Australia Pty. Ltd
4 Lentara Court
Cheltenham, Victoria, 3193 Australia
Email: ausadmin@halleonard.com

Visit Hal Leonard Online at
www.halleonard.com

Visit Phillip at
www.phillipkeveren.com

CHARLIE BROWN THEME

By VINCE GUARALDI
Arranged by Phillip Keveren

CHRISTMAS IS COMING

By VINCE GUARALDI
Arranged by Phillip Keveren

Bright Latin Rock (♩ = 96)

CHARLIE'S BLUES

By VINCE GUARALDI
Arranged by Phillip Keveren

CHRISTMAS TIME IS HERE

Words by LEE MENDELSON
Music by VINCE GUARALDI
Arranged by Phillip Keveren

FRIEDA
(With the Naturally Curly Hair)

By VINCE GUARALDI
Arranged by Phillip Keveren

THE GREAT PUMPKIN WALTZ

By VINCE GUARALDI
Arranged by Phillip Keveren

Jazz Waltz (♩ = 152)

HAPPINESS THEME

By VINCE GUARALDI
Arranged by Phillip Keveren

With a touch of melancholy, rubato (♩ = c. 96)

IT WAS A SHORT SUMMER, CHARLIE BROWN

By VINCE GUARALDI
Arranged by Phillip Keveren

LINUS AND LUCY

By VINCE GUARALDI
Arranged by Phillip Keveren

LOVE WILL COME

By VINCE GUARALDI
Arranged by Phillip Keveren

Expressively, with rubato (♩ = c. 69)

OH, GOOD GRIEF

By VINCE GUARALDI
Arranged by Phillip Keveren

THE PEBBLE BEACH THEME

By VINCE GUARALDI
Arranged by Phillip Keveren

To Coda ⊕

SURFIN' SNOOPY

By VINCE GUARALDI
Arranged by Phillip Keveren

YOU'RE IN LOVE, CHARLIE BROWN

By VINCE GUARALDI
Arranged by Phillip Keveren

SKATING

By VINCE GUARALDI
Arranged by Phillip Keveren